Spotlight on Colorado

GOVERNING THE CENTENNIAL STATE

Stephen Fienstein

PowerKiDS
press™

NEW YORK

Published in 2016 by The Rosen Publishing Group, Inc.
29 East 21st Street, New York, NY 10010

Book Design: Iron Cupcake Design

Cataloging-in-Publication Data

Names: Fienstein, Stephen.
Title: Governing the centennial state / Stephen Fienstein.
Description: New York : PowerKids Press, 2016. | Series: Spotlight on Colorado | Includes index.
Identifiers: ISBN 9781499415131 (pbk.) | ISBN 9781499415148 (6 pack) | ISBN 9781499415162 (library bound)
Subjects: LCSH: Colorado--Juvenile literature. | United States--Politics and government--Juvenile literature.
Classification: LCC F776.3 F54 2016 | DDC 978.8--dc23

Photo Credits: Ambient Ideas/Shutterstock.com, cover; Images by Dr. Alan Lipkin/Shutterstock.com, 3; Doug Pensinger/Getty Images, 5; Arina P Habich/Shutterstock.com, 6; EdgeOfReason/Shutterstock.com, 7; David Smart/Shutterstock.com, 8; Daderot/File:Signing of the Constitution by Albert Herter - Wisconsin Supreme Court - DSC03179.JPG/Wikimedia Commons, 10; Jeffrey M. Frank/Shutterstock.com, 11; Everett Historical/Shutterstock.com, 11; Orhan Cam/Shutterstock.com, 13; fstockfoto/Shutterstock.com, 14; Steve Petteway, Collection of the Supreme Court of the United States/Roberts Court (2010-) - The Oyez Project/File:Supreme Court US 2010.jpg/Wikimedia Commons, 15; kojihirano/Shutterstock.com, 16; William Morris./Natural Earth and Portland State University/File:Louisiana Purchase.png/Wikimedia Commons, 17; LC-DIG-pga-00517/Library of Congress, 18; DEA PICTURE LIBRARY/De Agostini Picture Library/Getty Images, 19; f11photo/Shutterstock.com, 21; Jeffrey M. Frank/Shutterstock.com, 23; AP Photo/Brennan Linsley, 24; Shaun Stanley/The Durango Herald via AP, 25; Andre Nantel/Shutterstock.com, 27; AP Photo/Ed Andrieski, 29; Nagel Photography/Shutterstock.com, 31; Doug Pensinger/Getty Images, 33; Matt McClain/Getty Images, 34; AP Photo/David Zalubowski, 35; AP Photo/David Zalubowski, 37; AP Photo/Brennan Linsley, 39; Arina P Habich/Shutterstock.com, 41; Neil Podoll/Shutterstock.com, 42; Mike Johnston/Cropped from File:Denver Mayor Michael Hancock - 2012-08-15.jpg by uploader; original from Flickr: DSC05681/File:Denver Mayor Michael Hancock - 2012-08-15 (portrait crop).jpg/Wikimedia Commons, 43; Bridget Calip/Shutterstock.com, 45.

Manufactured in the United States of America

CPSIA Compliance Information: Batch #BS15PK: For further information contact Rosen Publishing, New York, New York at 1-800-237-9932

Contents

CHAPTER 1

Why We Need Government

What does **government** mean to you? Whenever you hear that word, do you ever think about what role the government plays in your life? The government is not just a faraway, mysterious "thing" that has no connection to you or your family and friends. The government, in fact, is the group of people who have the authority to rule a **society**. And a society is made up of all the people who live in a town or city, a state, or a country. You are part of the society making up your town. You also belong to the society of your state and the society of the United States.

The government makes and carries out the laws and policies for the society. Every country has a government. But different countries around the world have different types of governments. Some countries, like

The idea of democracy is very old. It began in ancient Greece about 2,500 years ago.

John Hickenlooper became Colorado's governor in 2011.

the United States, are **democracies**, some are dictatorships, and others are monarchies. In our American democracy, we the people share in guiding the activities of the government. We do this by voting for our government representatives.

There are different kinds of monarchs in the world today. Some examples include the queen of England, the emperor of Japan, and the king of Saudi Arabia. Do you think a monarch would be good for the United States?

Although not all governments are the same, all governments must protect their **citizens** by maintaining the nation's security and providing law and order. Without law and order, you would not be safe. Ordinary activities of life, such as going to school, shopping at the mall, or doing a job would be difficult or even dangerous. Governments must also provide public services, such as mail delivery through the U.S. Postal Service.

National mail and postal service are provided by the United States government. This post office is located in Georgetown, Colorado.

Denver is Colorado's capital city. It is also the largest city in the state.

In addition to the federal government in Washington, D.C., state governments and local governments in each city, town, county, and village are responsible for a wide range of services to citizens in their areas. Among the most important of these are public education through the end of high school, emergency services and police and fire protection, health care, childcare, job training, low-cost housing, public parks, garbage collection, sewage treatment, and water, gas, and electricity utility services.

Think about all the things government does for us. Some people believe that we would be better off without the government providing so many services. They are afraid that government has grown too big and that private businesses could do a better job. What do you think?

CHAPTER 2

The United States Constitution

The U.S. government is based on law. But do you know where the laws of the land came from? Way back in 1787, the newly independent United States needed a plan of government. So 55 delegates from each of the 13 states except Rhode Island gathered in Independence Hall in Philadelphia to draw up the plan. The delegates, who would become known as the

FOUNDING FATHERS

Among the Founding Fathers in Philadelphia in 1787 were George Washington, James Madison, Alexander Hamilton, Benjamin Franklin, George Mason, and Robert Morris. Which of these names are familiar to you?

U.S. CONSTITUTION

Founding Fathers, then wrote the **Constitution**, the supreme law of the United States.

The Constitution, created in 1787 and ratified in 1788, came into force in 1789. The beginning, or Preamble, of the Constitution clearly spells out its purpose:

In the Constitution, the people grant the

"We the people of the United States, in order to form a more perfect union, establish justice, insure domestic tranquility, provide for the common defense, promote the general welfare, and secure the blessings of liberty to ourselves and our posterity, do ordain and establish this Constitution for the United States of America."

government limited powers to act on their behalf. The Founding Fathers established a system of shared power called federalism. The states keep certain powers while giving up other powers to a strong central government.

POPULAR SOVEREIGNTY

When the people consent to be governed and spell out the rules by which they will allow that governing to happen, this is called popular sovereignty. The power comes from the people—not a king, dictator, or president.

This mural shows the Founding Fathers signing the Constitution.

The seven Articles in the Constitution describe how the government is organized and how it works. To prevent any group in government from gaining too much authority, the Constitution divides the federal government into three branches—the **legislative branch**, the **executive branch**, and the **judicial branch**. You can see that the Founding Fathers were

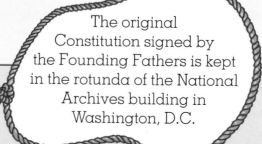

The original Constitution signed by the Founding Fathers is kept in the rotunda of the National Archives building in Washington, D.C.

very smart. They set up the federal government in a way that lets the three branches keep an eye on each other's powers and authority. This is a system of checks and balances.

The **amendment process** allows lawmakers to make changes or additions to the Constitution. Since 1788, several

Independence Hall is where the United States Constitution was signed.

thousand additions, called amendments, have been proposed, but only 27 were added to the Constitution. The first 10 amendments, which protect the rights of citizens from the power of the federal government, are called the Bill of Rights.

A LIVING DOCUMENT

Because the Constitution can be amended, think of it as a living document that can change with the times. For example, on January 31, 1865, about two months before the end of the Civil War, Congress passed the Thirteenth Amendment, which abolished slavery in the United States.

CHAPTER 3

Powers of the Federal Government

Congress, the legislative or lawmaking branch of the federal government, meets in the Capitol Building in Washington, D.C. Congress has two houses or chambers—the Senate and the House of Representatives. The American people vote for the members of Congress to represent them in the government. The Constitution gives Congress specific powers. Members of Congress rely on the Constitution to tell them the kinds of laws they can and can't pass. Some of the other powers of Congress include raising and spending money, declaring war, and regulating trade.

The executive branch of the federal government is led by the president and vice president. This branch carries out the laws made by Congress. The president must sign a **bill** sent to him by Congress before it can

Nearly 3 million people work in several hundred government departments and agencies of the executive branch. Their jobs include helping to arrange trade with other nations, improving the transportation of people and goods, protecting our natural resources, and developing new technologies to help agriculture, energy, and public health.

U.S. CAPITOL

become law. He has the power to **veto** or reject any bill he doesn't approve of. The president makes foreign policy, deciding how America will deal with other nations. He has the power to make treaties. As commander in chief of America's military forces, the president makes major military decisions in wartime. He also has the power to enforce the laws, grant pardons, and appoint certain officials.

The United States Supreme Court building

The judicial branch of the federal government protects the rights of all Americans. The federal Supreme Court, district courts, and appeals courts work together to ensure equal justice for all citizens. These courts protect the Constitution, and they apply the laws established by Congress. The federal

KNOWLEDGE NUGGET

Judges Appointed for Life

Justices of the Supreme Court, judges in the courts of appeals, judges in the district courts, and judges of the Court of International Trade are all appointed by the president and confirmed by the Senate. These judges are appointed for life and it is very hard for them to lose their jobs.

The Supreme Court of the United States has one chief justice and eight associate justices.

courts say what a law means and explain how that law applies to the facts in a particular case.

The United States Supreme Court is the most powerful court in the country. It is the court of appeal whose decisions are final. The Supreme Court can choose the cases it will hear. It has the power of judicial review—the power to decide whether acts of governments—national, state, or local—conflict with the Constitution.

The nine justices of the Supreme Court

CHAPTER 4

Government Comes to Colorado

Anasazi cliff dwellings at Mesa Verde

For thousands of years, the mountains and plains of what is now Colorado were home to various Native American peoples. These include the Anasazi, who built the first settlements, and later the Ute, Arapaho, Cheyenne, Comanche, and Navajo peoples. Explorers from Spain arrived in Colorado in the 1500s, and explorers from France in the 1600s. The Spanish and French had a long tug-of-war over Colorado. The United States bought eastern and central Colorado from France as part of the Louisiana Purchase in 1803. As a result of the Mexican-American War in 1848, the western part of Colorado also became part of the United States.

Major Stephen H. Long led an expedition across eastern Colorado in 1820. He called the vast rolling plains the "Great American Desert." He said crops would never be grown there. How wrong he was! Later, settlers turned the area into the "Breadbasket of the World."

As this map shows, the Louisiana Purchase included the eastern half of Colorado.

In 1858, everything changed. Gold was discovered west of what is now Denver. Thousands of gold seekers came to the area. Mining towns sprang up overnight in the mountains. As the population grew quickly, the new arrivals realized that something was missing—there was no government. Who would provide for their safety? Who would protect their property? Something needed to be done quickly.

MINER'S MEETINGS AND CLAIM CLUBS

In the new mining towns in the mountains, residents of each district participated in miners' meetings. They passed laws, set up a court, and elected officers—president, judge, sheriff, surveyor, and a recorder. In the farming communities, farmers formed claim clubs. Land claims of members were filed, identifying who owned or claimed parcels of land until a regular government was established.

DENVER 1859

In 1859, Coloradans set up their own government. They began to pass laws and elect officers, even though they lacked authority from the U.S. Congress to do so. They asked Congress to recognize Colorado as the Jefferson Territory. Congress refused. But in 1861 President James Buchanan signed a bill naming the area the Colorado Territory.

In 1864, the U.S. Congress passed an act giving the people of the Colorado Territory the right to enter the Union. First they had to write a constitution and vote to agree on it. The people voted against statehood. Why did this

DENVER 1876

happen? Well, today many people do not like to pay taxes. And back in 1864, people were no different. Many Coloradans at the time did not want to pay taxes to support a state government.

However, 10 years later, opinions changed. At the Constitutional Convention of 1874, the state constitution was created. Coloradans voted in favor of the constitution on July 1, 1876. And one month later, on August 1, President Ulysses S. Grant proclaimed Colorado a state of the Union. Colorado became the 38th state to be admitted to the United States.

THE CENTENNIAL STATE

Colorado's nickname is the Centennial State. In 1876, the United States was celebrating its centennial. This means the nation's 100th birthday since it declared its independence from Great Britain.

19

CHAPTER 5

Colorado's Constitution

In December 1874, 39 delegates from all over the Colorado Territory met in Denver to attend the Constitutional Convention. They accomplished their goal of writing Colorado's Constitution in 85 days. But heated debates, mainly over four important issues in the Constitution, continued until March 14, 1876, when the convention ended. The main arguments concerned taxation of church property, giving women the right to vote, state aid to church schools, and whether to mention God in the Preamble to the Constitution.

As in the United States Constitution, the Preamble tells the purpose of Colorado's Constitution. The Colorado Constitution calls for a government with the same structure as the federal government and that of other states. There are three branches: legislative, executive, and judicial. The state legislature consists of two houses—a senate and a house

The Colorado Constitution in 1876 was very long. It had about 23,000 words compared to the 4,543 words of the U.S. Constitution, before its 27 amendments were added.

COLORADO STATE CAPITOL BUILDING IN DENVER

of representatives. The chief executive is the governor. And the judicial branch consists of the state supreme court as well as several lower courts.

There are 27 articles in the Colorado Constitution. (There used to be 29, but two were done away with.) Colorado's bill of rights is in Article 2. Like the United States Constitution, the Colorado Constitution is a living document. It can be amended by the citizens of Colorado. Indeed, it has been amended 155 times.

The Preamble to the Colorado Constitution is similar to that of the United States Constitution in many ways. But while the Colorado Constitution pays its respect to the "Supreme Ruler of the Universe," there is no mention of God in the United States Constitution.

CHAPTER 6

The Executive Branch and the Governor

How would you like to work in a big office with a beautiful view out the window of the snowcapped Rocky Mountains? Well, this is where you would spend much of your time, in the State Capitol building in Denver, if you were the governor of Colorado. As governor, you would be the chief executive of the Centennial State's government, the highest officer of the state. According to the Colorado Constitution, you would possess the "supreme executive power of the state." However, like the governors of most states, your executive powers would be limited. You would actually often have to share your decision-making power with other officials, including the secretary of state, attorney general, state treasurer, and other officials.

Colorado is the only state to have three governors serve in a single day. On March 17, 1905, Alva Adams won the election. But the legislature quickly declared his opponent James Peabody governor on the condition that he immediately resign (leave office). Peabody's lieutenant governor Jesse McDonald then became governor.

Inside the Colorado State Capitol building. Colorado's governor has an office here.

Colorado's governor and the lieutenant governor are elected to a four-year term. A governor can serve up to two terms consecutively. Three other officials of the executive branch—the secretary of state, the attorney general, and the treasurer—are also elected by the voters to four-year terms, with a maximum of two terms. Directors of other executive branch departments are appointed by the governor.

COLORADO'S GOVERNORS

What kinds of people do you think became Colorado governors? It might surprise you to learn that some of Colorado's governors were miners, farmers, ranchers, newspapermen, a geologist who became a restaurant owner, and a district attorney.

The governor has several important official duties. These include signing bills, appointing people to office, and making a budget for the state. The governor has the power to veto a bill he or she does not approve of. The governor also has many unofficial activities to keep him or her busy. These include various kinds of public relations activities, ceremonial functions, welcoming conventions, and speaking in support of charities such as the March of Dimes.

If you lived in Colorado, what would you want your governor to do? Well, Coloradans

Governor John Hickenlooper sometimes visits schools, such as this elementary school in Denver.

Here Governor Hickenlooper talks to the press about two bills he signed into laws in 2015.

expect a lot of their governor. They expect him or her to balance the budget, improve highways, upgrade higher education, help create new jobs, help recruit new businesses, reduce crime, protect the environment, and plan for Colorado's future. He or she must also respond to emergencies or natural disasters—forest fires, floods, blizzards, droughts, prison riots, and high school shootings.

THE LIEUTENANT GOVERNOR

Colorado's governor has an awful lot on his or her plate. But what about the lieutenant governor, the person who is said to be "only a heartbeat away" from being governor? Although the lieutenant governor is the second-highest officer in the state, he or she actually has almost nothing to do, except for two basic duties. He or she must act as governor when the governor is out of state, and succeed the governor if he or she dies, retires, or is removed from office.

CHAPTER 7

The Legislative Branch

The legislative branch has the same structure as that of the federal government's legislative branch. This means that there are two houses in Colorado's legislative branch—the senate and the house of representatives. The senate has thirty-five members, and the house of representatives has 65 members. Colorado's voters elect senators to four-year terms. Representatives are elected to two-year terms. Both senators and representatives are limited to eight consecutive years in office.

The members of the legislative branch meet in a formal session for only four months a year. During this short time, they have a lot of work to accomplish. Among their jobs are making laws that support public education, building state parks and highways, setting salaries for

Senators and representatives often meet with their voters. They hold open houses or town meetings in their home communities. This is how they can learn about the concerns and interests of their voters.

The Colorado Senate meets in this room.

state officials, overseeing state programs, and holding investigations. They also play a role in the state budget process. So what do you think the state senators and representatives do the rest of the year? Most of them work in other professions.

KEEPING AN EYE ON THE GOVERNOR

In Washington, D.C., the executive branch is in the White House and the legislative branch is in the Capitol building. In Colorado, the state senators and representatives work in the same building as the governor—the state capitol building in Denver. Since the governor's powers are limited in many ways, perhaps this is a good idea. From the second floor, the members of the general assembly can keep an eye on the governor, whose office is down on the first floor.

While making the laws is one of the state legislators' most important jobs, the other job is acting as the representative of the voters who elected them to office. They often carry out this responsibility throughout the year, even while working at another job.

During each session of the Colorado legislature (known as the general assembly), all proposed new bills are discussed in **committees**. There are 10 committees in the house and 10 in the senate. Each committee, known as a committee of reference, has a different responsibility, for example, education, transportation, finance, health and human services, natural resources. Committee meetings are open to the public. Citizens have the opportunity to express their views on proposed bills. The committee then votes on the bill.

KNOWLEDGE NUGGET

Colorado has the only state legislature in the United States that cannot raise taxes without a vote by the people. Since tax increases have to be approved by the voters rather than the legislative branch, in a way it seems as if every Colorado voter is a government budget official.

COMMITTEE MEETING IN DENVER

WOMEN OF THE LEGISLATIVE BRANCH

In the 2011–12 session of the Colorado state legislature, women held 41 of the 100 seats. Colorado had the highest percentage of women in any state legislature in the United States. Three of the women were Hispanic, and one was African American.

CHAPTER 8

The Judicial Branch and Colorado's Courts

The judicial branch of Colorado's government consists of several courts. It includes the state supreme court, which is the highest court in the state. It also includes courts for different counties and districts within Colorado as well as **municipal** courts in the larger cities and towns. The state supreme court consists of a chief justice (judge) and six associate justices. They are appointed by the governor to serve a 10-year term. Justices may serve additional 10-year terms, but Colorado's voters must approve them each time. The governor appoints judges on the district courts and county courts. Municipal court judges are usually appointed by the town council or mayor.

Most of the laws under which Coloradans live are the laws of the state. State

What is one big difference between Colorado's judicial branch and the judicial branch of the federal government? The federal justices and judges are appointed for life. The Colorado justices are not. Which system do you think is better?

judges apply the state bill of rights to many of the most important legal matters in people's lives. The state and municipal judges deal with more local issues.

Although people do not always agree with court decisions, in general Coloradans are satisfied with their state court system. In 2010, a statewide poll found a two-to-one approval rating for Colorado's courts.

Have you ever heard of water courts and water judges? Colorado has special courts devoted to water. There are seven water courts, one in each of the seven major river basins in Colorado. The seven river basins are the South Platte, Arkansas, Rio Grande, Gunnison, Colorado, White, and San Juan. In Colorado, some of the most heated arguments arise over water rights and the use of water. Should certain water users have

Supreme court in Denver

preference over other water users? Who has legitimate rights to a particular source of water, and who does not? These issues result in some of the longest-drawn-out cases in Colorado's courts.

CHAPTER 9

Voting Rights in Colorado

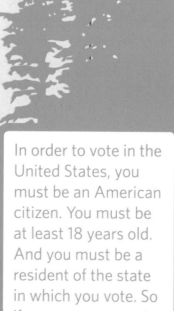

Someday you will be old enough to vote. Voting is an important responsibility of every American citizen. You are a citizen of the United States, a citizen of your home state, and a citizen of your city or town. As a citizen, you owe allegiance to your government. In exchange for that loyalty, you are entitled to government protection. Citizens have certain rights and responsibilities. Perhaps the most important of these is the right and responsibility to vote. After all, voting is the most powerful tool you have for influencing your government. Your vote tells people in government what you think and feel.

Before you can take part in an election, you must be registered to vote. **Registration** is the process of signing up to vote in the district or area where you live. Today in Colorado there is a quick and easy way to register online

In order to vote in the United States, you must be an American citizen. You must be at least 18 years old. And you must be a resident of the state in which you vote. So if you want to vote in Colorado, you must have been a citizen of Colorado for at least 22 days before the election.

You can also choose not to register in any political party. In that case, you will be registered as "unaffiliated." About one-third of Colorado's voters choose to register as unaffiliated.

These banners advertised the Democratic National Convention, held in Denver in 2008. This was an important meeting for members of the Democratic Party, one of two major political parties in the United States.

when you are 18 years of age. Coloradans may register in one of the two major **political parties**, Republican or Democratic. They can also register in one of the minor third parties, such as the Libertarian Party, the Green Party, or the American Constitution Party.

In Colorado and in every other state, Election Day takes place on the Tuesday after the first Monday in November. National elections are held along with state and local elections. On the ballot, you will see candidates' names for such offices as president and vice president, senator, congressional representative, governor, state house member, state senator, mayor, judge, and board member. The ballot may also contain questions for you to decide on a variety of issues.

Every registered voter in Colorado can now vote by mail. You receive the ballot in the mail, fill it out, and mail it in. You can also vote in person. To do this, go to the nearest voting service and polling center. There you will either use a touch-screen voting machine or a voting machine that uses a wheel. There will also be accessible voting machines for voters with disabilities.

MOTOR VOTER REGISTRATION

Colorado and several other states have a convenient way to get younger citizens and newcomers to the state to get registered to vote. Whenever you obtain or renew your driver's license, you will automatically be asked if you want to register to vote. This is called "motor voter" registration.

Of course, you will cast your votes in secret. You never write or sign your name on a ballot. No one in the polling center may ask you how you voted. This is one of our most important freedoms.

Some voting booths use modern technology like iPads.

Unfortunately, many Americans who are eligible to vote choose not to do so. Some people don't trust the candidates who are running for office. Some are turned off by negative campaigns. Others feel that the government is not effective and doesn't represent their point of view. It is important to be informed about the candidates and the issues in an election, so that you know who and what you are voting for. Always remember, your vote counts!

COLORADO'S WOMEN WIN THE RIGHT TO VOTE

A very important issue was on the ballot in the general election in Colorado on November 7, 1893. Colorado's male electorate voted on a women's suffrage bill, a bill giving Colorado's women the right to vote. The election returns were 35,698 votes for the bill and 29,461 against. Colorado became the second state granting women the right to vote. Wyoming had been first, in 1890.

Constitutional amendments can also become law by a two-thirds vote in both houses of the Colorado legislature. But this method is more difficult to accomplish than the initiative process.

CHAPTER 10:

Direct Democracy in Colorado

Citizens of Colorado exercise their democratic rights to participate in government by voting for the candidates of their choice to represent them in government. But there is another way in which citizens can become more directly involved. Suppose there is a particular issue about which Coloradans feel very strongly. And what if Colorado's state government has not gotten around to dealing with that issue. Citizens can then take direct action to bring a bill before their elected representatives in Colorado's general assembly.

Here's how **direct democracy** works. Coloradans can propose a new law through the **citizen initiative process**—starting a bill on their own. They then ask other voters to sign a **petition** to show their agreement. If the required number of voters signs the petition, it becomes a proposition, or proposed law. It then either passes through the legislative process in

In 2000, Colorado's voters approved an initiated constitutional amendment allowing marijuana to be provided to medical patients in order to relieve pain. Then in 2014, another amendment legalized the sale of marijuana to any adult 21 and older, making Colorado the first state to do so.

Colorado's general assembly or appears in the next election on a ballot for the state's voters to decide. The vote for or against an item on the ballot is called a referendum.

The reason that Colorado's Constitution is so long is that it is easy to initiate a constitutional amendment. Over the years, the Constitution has grown longer and longer as Coloradans made frequent use of the initiative process to put new ideas and programs into the Constitution. Many important changes were made to the Colorado Constitution by initiated amendments.

The citizen initiative process was first adopted in Colorado in 1910. In the battle for its adoption, the state's Democrats were in favor of the process and the Republicans were against it. At the time, Colorado's Democratic governor John F. Shafroth believed that if citizens could initiate laws and constitutional amendments, this would make state legislators more careful and accountable.

These students are protesting too much standardized testing in Colorado schools.

CHAPTER 11

Political Parties in Colorado

You have probably heard of the two main political parties in the United States. They are the Democratic Party and the Republican Party. Most elected officials in the federal, state, and local governments throughout the country belong to one of these main political parties. Other political parties also exist, such as the Green Party and Libertarian Party.

Do you know what political parties do? In Colorado, as in other states, political parties do the following jobs: They choose and support candidates for all elected political offices. They work to elect their candidates to office. They develop a political platform, which explains what the party thinks about important issues. And they educate and try to influence citizens on policies and issues.

Colorado's Republican and Democratic parties nominate their candidates at primary elections held in June before the November

The United States Constitution makes no mention of political parties. Yet soon after the writing of the Constitution, the two-party system of government began to take shape.

Governor John Hickenlooper is a member of the Democratic party.

election. A complicated system of caucuses (meeting of party members) and conventions are used to narrow the field of candidates that eventually run against each other in the primary elections.

Colorado has had more Democratic than Republican governors. Today there is an almost equal balance between Democratic, Republican, and unaffiliated (those not belonging to a party) registered voters in Colorado.

The role of political parties in Colorado as in other places can be very complicated. But when you think about it, there cannot be any politics without political parties. And without politics, there is no democracy. Do you agree with this idea?

CHAPTER 12

Local Government

Colorado is different from most other states in one surprising way. Its local governments are more powerful than the state government. In fact, Colorado has one of the weakest state governments in the country. So how did this situation come about? Well, back in 1904, an amendment to Colorado's Constitution gave Denver the right to establish a "home rule" city government. This was followed by another amendment giving strong home-rule powers to other Colorado cities. "Home rule" means that Colorado's cities and towns were no longer under the thumb of the state government.

Colorado has almost 2,000 local governments. Each of the following has a local government: more than 250 cities and towns,

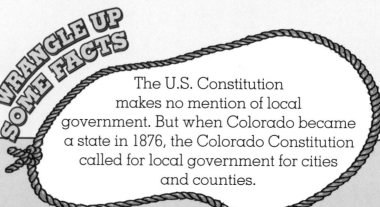

WRANGLE UP SOME FACTS

The U.S. Constitution makes no mention of local government. But when Colorado became a state in 1876, the Colorado Constitution called for local government for cities and counties.

WALSH LIBRARY IN OURAY, COLORADO

64 counties, and about 1,500 special districts for fire departments, schools, libraries, and other services. According to one state government official, Colorado is more a collection of powerful local governments than a state ruled by a state government.

Colorado Springs is a city of over 400,000 people.

The various levels of local government provide many services for Colorado's citizens. The most important involve education, public safety, health and welfare, environment and housing, land use through zoning rules, and utilities. Of course, this all costs money—a lot of money. So how do local governments pay for the services they provide? If you guessed through property taxes, you'd be right. But federal and state governments often give money to local governments to help support services that are state or national priorities.

Although many Coloradans believe that the state has too many governments, most local governments have the strong support of residents of the state's cities and towns. Do you think a strong state government would be better for Colorado than a huge number of powerful local governments?

Some Colorado cities, such as Denver and Colorado Springs, have a local government with a strong mayor. The mayor is elected, often by the voters, to preside over city council meetings. The state's other cities have the council-manager form of government. The city manager, hired by the city council, runs the city. The city council enacts the city's laws

Denver mayor Michael Hancock

and policies, and the city manager enforces the laws and carries out the policies.

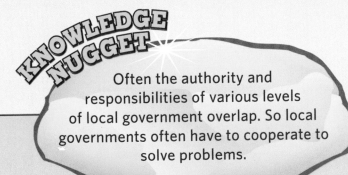

Often the authority and responsibilities of various levels of local government overlap. So local governments often have to cooperate to solve problems.

CHAPTER 13

Colorado's Education System

Imagine that you were living in the little town of Auraria in Colorado back in 1860. (That year, Auraria, located just west of Cherry Creek, would become part of the new city of Denver on the east side of the creek.) Coloradans had set up their first government the previous year in 1859. And some people in the government were beginning to think about the need to create a system of education.

A man called O.J. Goldrick opened a school in Auraria—Colorado's first public school. Goldrick's school was very small. In fact, it was in a little log cabin. It began with just over a dozen students. Mr. Goldrick picked up the students individually in his horse-drawn wagon.

Providing free public K–12 education for the state's children is one of the most important jobs of Colorado's government. In 1948, the Colorado Constitution was amended to provide for an elected state board of education.

In 1865, the superintendent position was abolished by law, and the territorial treasurer was given the responsibility for Colorado's schools. This job didn't pay very much. The treasurer's salary was $100 per year. In 1870, the public instruction position was reinstated, and the salary was $1,000 per year.

Public education in Colorado is free, but it costs a lot of money to run the state's schools. Teachers must be paid and school property must be maintained. There are other expenses, such as providing school buses to transport children to school. The money for these expenses comes from taxes.

Early one-room schoolhouse in Colorado

All levels of government—federal, state, and local—are involved in various ways with public education. And governments raise the necessary funding from taxes. Coloradans pay taxes based on how much property they own to their local governments. And they pay taxes based on how much money they make to the state and federal governments.

From its small beginning in a single log cabin in 1860, Colorado's Department of Education has grown into a huge system. Today the Department of Education includes 1,780 public schools in 178 school districts. At least 840,000 students attend the state's public schools. And 130,000 educators work in these schools. So no matter where you might live in Colorado, a public school is available for you.

Glossary

amendment process—the rules that allow lawmakers to make changes or additions to the Constitution

bill—a proposed law presented for approval to a legislative body

citizen initiative process—a way for citizens to propose a new law by starting a bill on their own

citizens—people who owe allegiance to a government and who are entitled to government protection

committee—a working group of legislators established to solve a problem or series of issues

Congress—the legislative branch of the federal or state governments, consisting of two houses—the Senate and the House of Representatives

Constitution—the document that contains the plan of government of a country or state

democracy—a society in which the people vote for the officials who will represent them in the government

direct democracy—a system of government in which citizens vote directly for the laws by which they will be ruled

executive branch—the part of the federal or state governments that carries out the laws

government—the group of people who have the authority to rule a society

judicial branch—the part of the federal or state governments that interprets the laws

legislative branch—the lawmaking part of the federal or state governments

municipal—relating to a city or town

petition—a formal written request of an authority concerning a particular issue or cause

political parties—groups of citizens organized to promote and support specific ideas for government and candidates for public office

registration—the process of signing up to vote

society—all the people who live in a town, city, state, or country

veto—the power to prevent a bill that has passed the legislature from becoming law

Index

Due to the changing nature of Internet links, the Rosen Publishing Group, Inc., has developed an online list of websites related to the subject of this book. This site is updated regularly. Please use this link to access the list:
http://www.powerkidslinks.com/soco/gcs